HIP-HOP
Biographies

CHRIS
BROWN

SADDLEBACK
PUBLISHING

HIP-HOP Biographies

Chris Brown
Drake
50 Cent
Jay-Z
Nicki Minaj

Pitbull
Rihanna
Usher
Lil Wayne
Kanye West

SADDLEBACK
PUBLISHING
www.sdlback.com

ISBN-13: 978-162250-017-8
ISBN-10: 1-62250-017-2
eBook: 978-1-61247-698-8

Printed in Guangzhou, China
NOR/0713/CA21301256
17 16 15 14 13   2 3 4 5 6

Table of Contents

Timeline

2004: Island Def Jam Records offers Chris a contract. He turns it down.

Chris signs a contract with Jive Records.

1989: Chris Brown was born in Tappahannock, Virginia.

1991: Chris teaches himself to dance by imitating Michael Jackson.

2005: Chris releases his debut album, *Chris Brown*.

1996: Chris's parents divorce.

2006: Chris is nominated for two Grammy Awards.

2002: Chris is discovered by a music producer.

2007: Chris releases his second album, *Exclusive*.

2008: Chris wins the award for best singer at the Nickelodeon Kids' Choice Award.

Billboard names Chris Artist of the Year.

2009: Chris assaults girlfriend Rihanna.

A judge sentenced Chris to five years' *probation*.

Chris releases his third album, *Graffiti.*

2011: Chris releases his fourth album, *F.A.M.E.*

2012: Chris wins his first Grammy Award for Best R&B Album.

Chris releases his fifth album, *Fortune.*

Chris taught himself to dance by watching Michael Jackson.

A Young Dancer

Christopher Maurice Brown was born on May 5, 1989. He grew up in a small town, Tappahannock, Virginia. His mother, Joyce, worked in a day-care facility. Chris's father, Clinton, was a corrections officer at a nearby prison. He had an older sister, Tootie.

Chris remembers dancing as early as two years old. He would watch performers on television and copy their moves. He especially liked imitating Michael Jackson's moves. With help from his father, Chris learned Michael Jackson's famous moonwalk.

Chris would also listen to his parents' records. He grew up on soul music by artists from Sam Cooke to Teddy Pendergrass to Stevie Wonder.

Chris was not just focused on dancing. He also loved to sing. He would sing with his church choir. When his parents had people over for parties or cookouts, Chris would dance for them.

Tappahannock only had about 2,000 people. There were not a lot of opportunities for Chris to perform aside from church and at home. So his mother took him to talent shows in neighboring towns. Chris got a lot of attention from his dancing. He would add flips to his routines that he taught himself on his trampoline.

Then Chris discovered a new young artist named Usher. The young singer could dance the way Chris wanted to. He also had a great voice. So Chris focused on learning how to do everything Usher did.

Chris's parents divorced when he was seven years old. Soon his mother was in a new relationship. She married the man, who moved the family to a trailer park.

Unfortunately, Chris's stepfather was abusive. After Chris went to bed, his stepfather would hit Chris's mother. She tried to hide her injuries. She did not want her children to know what was happening.

But Chris knew what was going on. He was so scared of his stepfather that he would hide in his bed. Some nights Chris needed to use the restroom. But he refused to leave his bed. He was too scared. Chris would rather wet his bed than see his mother get hurt. The abuse lasted for five years.

The violence in Chris's home left him scared and shy. He often talked to his mother about what was happening to her. But she would not leave her husband. Chris continued dancing during this time. He would act confident and outgoing on stage, but inside he was scared.

When he was eleven, Chris had a conversation with his mother. He remembered telling her, "I just want you to know that I love you, but I'm gonna take a baseball bat one day while you are at work, and I'm gonna kill him."

Chris never acted on his threat. But his life did change. His stepfather shot himself in the head and blinded himself. Years later his mother would finally leave. But Chris never forgot the violence. He said, "It affected me, especially (my behavior) toward women. I treat them differently. I don't want to put a woman through the same thing that person put my mom through."

Chris learned to draw. He would play basketball with young men at the community center. He became a great ball player. When he was in sixth grade, he played for the school's eighth-grade team. Every day riding home on the school bus, the girls made him sing for them. Chris used all of these activities to stay away from the drama at home. He said, "Music, basketball, and drawing was my outlet to keep me away from all that."

Chris's mother knew he could dance. She knew he liked to sing in the choir. But in 2000 she discovered that her son had a great singing voice. Chris remembered, "I was eleven [in my house] and watching Usher perform 'My Way,' and I started trying to mimic it. My mom was like, 'You can sing?' And I was like, 'Well, yeah, Mama.' "

Then in 2002 a producer from Hitmission Records was in Tappahannock. The company sent producers around the country to find new talent. They saw Chris sing and dance and were interested in working with him. The company gave Chris a voice coach. Then they helped Chris make a *demo*. He called himself C-Swizzle.

Chris was then introduced to T.J. Allen, another young musician. T.J.'s father was a record producer. Chris traveled to New York City to work with T.J. Then he returned home so he could keep up with his classes. Finally Chris decided to finish school at home and focus on his music career with T.J. He moved to New York City.

Chris mimicked how Usher sang and danced.

Meeting Tina Davis

T.J.'s father had the two boys make a demo. He sent it to record companies, including Island Def Jam. Tina Davis was a vice president in A&R with the company. She liked the demo and Chris's voice. She said, "The first thing that hit me was his unique voice. I thought this kid is a star." Tina took them to meet L.A. Reid, the company's CEO. T.J. and Chris performed for him. The boys were offered a contract right away. Chris was thrilled. He remembered, "I called my mom about to cry, but I was like, 'No, I'm a boy. I'm not supposed to cry.'"

Unfortunately, Island Def Jam's offer was not a good deal for the boys. Tina saw what was happening. She warned Chris that they were being offered a bad deal. Chris said, "They took care of me this whole time, and then they started being snakes." The boys walked out.

Tina was fired from Island Def Jam. The day she lost her job, she called Chris. She offered to be his manager, and he accepted. She moved Chris and T.J. into her New Jersey home. Chris remembered, "We thought she was super rich! She lived in a regular neighborhood, and we was from the ghetto. We was wearing a whole bunch of dirty clothes. She would buy us fresh things every week, new sneakers."

Chris hired Tina Davis as his manager.

Tina worked with the boys so they would not be taken advantage of. She told them about singers who were cheated by bad contracts. She did not want this to happen to Chris and T.J. Tina also gave the boys lessons in manners. They needed to know how to behave in public.

Davis represented each singer separately rather than as a pair. She had Chris make a video of himself performing. She also had him make more demos. She took the music to Jive Records, HitQuarters, and Warner Brothers Records. The companies were very interested. One HitQuarters executive remembered, "I saw the potential ... I didn't love all the records, but I loved his voice."

Island Def Jam was still interested. L.A. Reid asked Usher to call Chris and convince him to sign with him. Chris remembered, "Usher called me right before I got signed and he was like, 'Whatever you do, just make sure it's the best thing for you and it benefits you 100 percent.' He was very influential to me. I was like, 'Thank you, bro. I'm still not signing with [Reid].'"

Finally in 2004 Chris and Tina decided to sign with Jive Records. Chris said, "I picked Jive because they had the best success with younger artists in the pop market. ... I knew I was going to capture my African American audience, but Jive had a lot of strength in the pop area as well as longevity in careers." Jive had great success with artists like Justin Timberlake and Britney Spears when they were teens like Chris.

Jive lined up great songwriters for Chris, including Jermaine Dupri and Scott Storch. They also had him move away from rap. Tina and the people at Jive understood that Chris would be more successful as a soul singer. Chris finally agreed. He said, "I figured that my voice was unique and that girls were more attracted to the voice."

Chris signed with Jive Records because they worked with other young artists like Justin Timberlake and Britney Spears.

At age fifteen, Chris was preparing to release his debut album. He started recording in February 2005. By May he had recorded fifty songs. Jive chose fourteen to appear on his album, entitled *Chris Brown.* Chris was co-writer of five of the songs. He said, "I write about the things that sixteen-year-olds go through every day, like you just got in trouble for sneaking your girl into the house, or you can't drive, so you steal a car or something."

The album would not be released until November of that year. Radio stations held concerts with many different artists performing just a few songs each. It gave the artists a chance to start building a fan base. So Chris performed at many radio station concerts while he was waiting for his album to come out. Sometimes he got paid to perform, but most of the time he did not. He just sang in exchange for the publicity.

Finally Chris's first single was released. He recorded Usher's "Yeah" with new lyrics. The song was called "Run It!" The song reached the number-one position on the *Billboard* Hot 100 charts. It had been over ten years since a male singer debuted in the number-one position.

The album reached number two on the *Billboard* 200 album charts. Chris put out a total of five singles from the album. It sold over three million copies around the world. Chris went on tour in Great Britain and Japan to help sell the album overseas. He was on his way to becoming a star. He said in an interview, "I hope I can be the next Michael Jackson."

Chris appeared on MTV's *Total Request Live.*

Singer, Dancer, Actor

The Grammy Award nominations came out in 2006. Chris was nominated for two awards, Best New Artist and Best R&B Contemporary Album. He lost the Best New Artist award to country singer and *American Idol* winner Carrie Underwood. Chris lost the album award to Beyoncé. But being nominated brought Chris even more attention. He was also asked to perform at the ceremony. He sang with soul legends Lionel Richie and Smokey Robinson.

After the Grammy Awards, Chris went to a party that Usher was hosting. Music was playing, and there was a dance floor. Chris took the opportunity to show Usher and his guests what he could do. Chris remembered, "I just went out there on the dance floor, did my thing and they ended up putting the cameras on me. I don't like to say it, but yeah, I stole the show that night."

Chris released a DVD called *Chris Brown's Journey.* It was filmed while he was on tour in Great Britain and Japan. It also showed him getting ready for the Grammy Awards.

Chris was also invited to act on television shows. He appeared on the sitcom *One on One* on the UPN Network. He also performed on the *Brandon T. Jackson Show.*

As a teen performer, Chris had many young fans. In 2007 he was nominated as the best singer at the Nickelodeon Kids' Choice Award. He won the award the next year. He also won the Teen Choice Award for Best Male Artist.

Chris was named the Best Male Artist at the Teen Choice Awards.

Chris made a lot of money on his first album and tour. He built a six-bedroom house back home in Virginia. He built his mother a house just like his down the street. He bought himself a Ford Expedition and a Lamborghini.

Even with the sudden riches, Tina tried to keep Chris's life as normal as possible. She said, "When he asks to go play basketball with his friends in Harlem, because that's what he loves, how could I say no? They treat him just like he's Chris Brown back then. And that's so important." She worked to keep people around him that would treat him like a teenage boy, not a star.

In 2007 Chris started recording his second album, *Exclusive*. He knew it was important to make this album at least as successful as the first. He said, "With a second album, there's a lot of pressure to maintain status. It's like if you're popular in high school, you gotta keep it up—keep the fresh gear on, keep saying the right things. The whole music industry is like high school. I guess prom was the Grammy's."

Chris was also able to meet one of his idols, Michael Jackson. They first met when Chris was performing in a tribute to Michael's hit album, *Thriller*. Chris remembered, "Michael said to me, 'being able to dance and sing; that's rare. Nobody can do it—only you, me and a couple of others. Keep working and dream big.'" Michael and Chris talked often about recording together. But because Michael died in 2009, it never happened.

Exclusive was released in November 2007. He earned his second *Billboard* Hot 100 number-one hit. The song "Kiss Kiss" featured rapper T-Pain. The album had two other hit singles, "With You" and "Forever." The album was number four on the *Billboard* 200 album charts. Again, he sold about three million albums around the world.

Chris was invited to perform at the 2007 MTV Video Music Awards. He was not expected to be the biggest news of the show. Britney Spears had experienced a huge setback in her career. Her performance at the show was a highly-anticipated comeback. But when she took the stage, she did not sing. Instead she lip-synced to her music. She stumbled on her words and danced poorly. The act that was supposed to be the hit of the show was a flop. Then Chris performed. He sang and danced his heart out. Justin Timberlake was in the audience. He reacted by saying, "Whatever Chris Brown just did, reminded me how much I'm getting older." Chris said in an interview later, "I just had a lot to prove. So when I got out there I was like, 'Lemme show you what I could really do.'"

Chris worked with St. Jude Children's Research Hospital. They cared for sick children. In 2007 they had a Math-a-Thon and Chris was the host. The program had kids use their math skills to help children with cancer.

Chris also started dating the singer Rihanna. She described him this way: "He's one of my closest friends in the industry. He makes me feel like a teenager. I have to act and think like an adult so much. He makes me feel young again."

Gaining Fame

The same year that Chris released his second album, he also appeared in his first movie. *Stomp the Yard* was a movie about street dancing and college dance crews. It was a great fit for Chris's talent.

Chris was on television too. He made a guest appearance on three episodes of the series *The O.C.* Chris said, "I play, like, a band geek—I'm really stepping out of my own character. I was kind of a geek in school, grade-wise. But style-wise, I was always popular and cool. But [on *The O.C.*] I'm geeked out all the way." He appeared as himself on *The Suite Life of Zack and Cody.* He also acted in the television movie *This Christmas*.

As Chris became more famous, he found himself working with bigger stars. He performed with Jordin Sparks on her song, "No Air." Their song reached number three on the *Billboard* Hot 100. He sang on Ludacris's song, "What Them Girls Like." He worked with T-Pain on "Freeze." Chris went on tour in Australia with Beyoncé. Then Chris re-released *Exclusive* as *Exclusive: The Forever Edition.* This version had four new songs. The new single, "Forever," reached number two on the *Billboard* Hot 100. At the end of 2008 *Billboard* named Chris the Artist of the Year.

Chris was growing more and more famous. He saw what stars like Beyoncé were able to do. She was a great musician. But she also branched out into other businesses. Chris wanted to do the same. He said, "I wanna be a mogul. I wanna be a singer, actor, entrepreneur, have a clothing line, be an executive everything."

Chris Brown and Ne-Yo appeared in the movie *Stomp the Yard*.

The Wrigley Company hired Chris to *promote* their Doublemint gum. Chris appeared in an ad encouraging people to drink milk. He even appeared on *Sesame Street*.

Chris's relationship with Rihanna was going well too. Paparazzi caught them kissing when they were out to dinner. Chris told a reporter, "Our relationship is growing. We started off as friends and we're getting a little bit closer now."

Chris and Rihanna were both invited to perform at the Grammy Awards on February 8, 2009. A news story broke the day of the awards. Chris was being investigated for assaulting a woman. The Grammy organizers announced that he would not be performing. Neither would Rihanna. It did not take long for people to realize that she was the woman Chris assaulted.

Chris turned himself in to the police. A photo of Rihanna's battered face was leaked. It was shown in newspapers and on television around the world. Reporters were looking for any information about their relationship that they could find.

Reporters looked at the reports that were filed in the case. They discovered that the assault on Rihanna was not the first time Chris had been violent toward her. Chris had shoved her against a wall and smashed the windows of a car. Then on the night before the Grammy's, they had another argument in Los Angeles. Rihanna became upset that a woman was texting Chris. The message made it sound like Chris and the woman were romantically involved. The woman was supposedly Tina Davis.

Rihanna got upset and threw the car keys out the window. Chris reacted by choking, biting, and hitting Rihanna. He also threatened to kill her. She passed out and woke up with a black eye and bruises all over her face.

Chris was arrested for assaulting Rihanna.

Guilty

Chris turned himself in the evening of the assault. The police charged Chris with *felony* assault and making criminal threats. The public reacted strongly to Chris's arrest. Radio stations stopped playing his music. Wrigley and the Milk Board pulled his advertisements. *Sesame Street* stopped playing his segment with Elmo.

Chris stayed out of the spotlight. He sent a message to the press. He said, "Words cannot begin to express how sorry and saddened I am over what transpired." Then he posted a video on his website. He said, "I am very saddened and very ashamed of what I have done. I have told Rihanna countless times, and I am telling you today, that I am truly sorry and that I wasn't able to handle the situation both differently and better."

In June 2009 Chris pled guilty. He was sentenced to five years' probation, community service, and *domestic violence* counseling. The judge also ordered Chris to stay at least ten yards away from Rihanna whenever they were in public. At any other location, he had to stay fifty yards away.

A few months later, Chris appeared on *Larry King Live*. Chris talked about what he did: "I'm in shock, because, first of all, that's not who I am as a person, and that's not who I promise I want to be." He said about Rihanna, "I'm pretty sure we can always be friends, and I don't know about our relationship, but I just know definitely that we ended as friends."

Chris pled guilty for his attack on Rihanna.

Fan reactions to the assault were mixed. Many people were outraged by what Chris had done. Rihanna's fans were very upset by her being hurt. Chris had been very public about the abuse his mother went through when he was young. Now his critics said that he should have known how harmful domestic violence can be. Of all people, Chris should have known better.

But many of Chris's fans supported him, especially young girls. Many of them did not believe that Chris did anything to Rihanna. One said, "I thought she was lying, or that the tabloids were making it up." Others felt that it was Rihanna's fault that she was assaulted. A young female fan said, "She probably made him mad for him to react like that." A study was done in Boston. Of the teenagers asked, nearly half of them said that the assault was Rihanna's fault.

Teens' reaction toward the assault led to many changes. Organizations reached out to teens to teach them about dating violence. They worked hard to help boys and girls understand that it is never okay to be abused by a boyfriend or girlfriend. Even Oprah Winfrey dealt with teen dating violence on her show because of the assault.

Many of Chris's fans turned against Rihanna. Girls with crushes on Chris were unhappy he was dating anyone. When Chris was charged with assault, they sent Rihanna hateful Facebook and Twitter messages. Others posted ranting videos on YouTube. It was easier to be upset with Rihanna than to blame the cute star they had a crush on.

Many of Chris's fans were unwilling to believe he could be violent.

Chris started his community service in the middle of 2009. He cleaned graffiti off of buildings. He picked up trash on roads and pulled weeds. He stopped his community service before his six months was up so he could go back to recording.

In December 2009 Chris released his third album, *Graffiti*. The album was different in style than the earlier two albums. Chris explained, "I wanted to change it up and really be different. Like my style nowadays, I don't try to be typical urban. I want to be like how Prince, Michael and Stevie Wonder were. They can cross over to any genre of music."

The first single, "I Can Transform Ya," reached number twenty on the *Billboard* Hot 100. The song featured rappers Lil Wayne and Swizz Beatz. Chris released two more singles, "Crawl" and "Sing Like Me." But the album did not get very good reviews. It also sold poorly compared to his earlier albums.

Chris blamed music sellers for the poor sales. He said that stores were blackballing his music. In other words, he said that music stores refused to sell his music. He lashed out at Walmart, saying they "didn't even have my album in the back ... not on shelves, saw for myself." In fact, the store was not refusing to stock his music. They had actually sold out of his album.

Chris took to his Twitter account again and again to complain about stores not selling his music. Stores answered back that they were stocking the album. Worse, they were stuck with too many copies because it was not selling well. Finally Chris stopped responding by deleting his Twitter account for a short time.

Chris performed in the video for his song "Crawl."

Another Blowup

Chris's career suffered because of his conviction. In June 2009 the BET network had a televised tribute to Michael Jackson. Chris was supposed to perform. At the last minute, his act was cancelled. Sponsors complained about him being on the show. Chris thought BET was being hypocritical because other artists with criminal pasts could perform. He said, "I felt like BET should have been looking at the people who got drug charges, gun charges, weapons, other stuff. You can't discriminate against one person because you're afraid the media is going to kill you."

Chris watched the tribute to one of his idols from home. He thought it was terrible. He remembered, "I was watching it, holding my face, like 'Oh my God, this is wack.' I was expecting them to have Usher, Omarion and even Justin [Timberlake]. They were so bent on not getting me there that they messed up their own show."

Then Chris scheduled a European tour to promote *Graffiti*. But a judge in Great Britain refused to let him into the country. They felt that because he was convicted of a violent crime, they did not want him in the country. He had to postpone his tour.

In March 2011 Chris appeared on *Good Morning America* to promote his fourth album, *F.A.M.E.* In between songs, host Robin Roberts asked about his relationship with Rihanna. When the show went to commercial, Chris went to his dressing room. He was so angry that he broke a window. He yelled at a producer and security. Then he left the studio. He ranted to his fans about reporters bringing up his past. He later apologized for his behavior.

Chris performed on *Good Morning America* before losing his temper.

Chris struggled to get his career back on track. But he did find some successes. In June 2010 he was welcomed back to BET. They had another tribute to Michael Jackson during the BET Awards show. Chris performed a number of Michael's hits. He even wore Jackson's trademark sequined glove and moonwalked.

Then he sang Michael's "Man in the Mirror." While he was singing, Chris dropped to his knees and started to cry. The celebrities in the audience were very moved. Rapper Trey Songz said, "He left his heart on the stage. He gave genuine emotion. I was proud of him and I was happy for him for having that moment." Michael's brother Jermaine said, "It was very emotional for me, because it was an acceptance from his fans from what has happened to him and also paying tribute to my brother." And Chris said in a speech later, "I let y'all down before, but I won't do it again ... I promise."

Chris was able to perform his tribute to Michael Jackson.

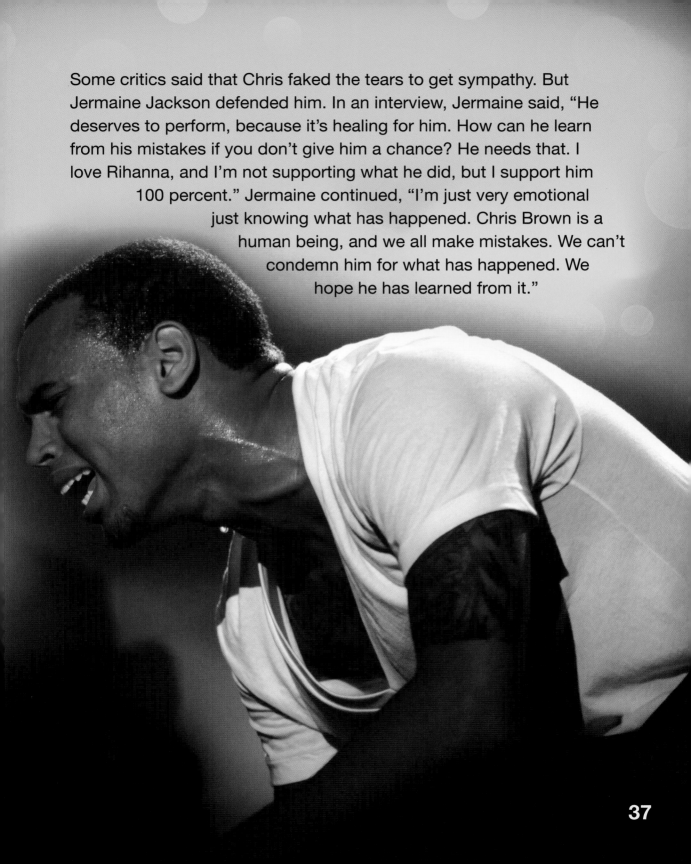

Some critics said that Chris faked the tears to get sympathy. But Jermaine Jackson defended him. In an interview, Jermaine said, "He deserves to perform, because it's healing for him. How can he learn from his mistakes if you don't give him a chance? He needs that. I love Rihanna, and I'm not supporting what he did, but I support him 100 percent." Jermaine continued, "I'm just very emotional just knowing what has happened. Chris Brown is a human being, and we all make mistakes. We can't condemn him for what has happened. We hope he has learned from it."

In December 2010 Chris completed his domestic violence course. He was very proud of himself. Chris *tweeted* his fans, "I have enough self-respect and decency to be proud of accomplishing this DV class. Boyz run from [their] mistakes. Men learn from them!!!"

Chris toured North America and Australia.

Chris's fourth album, *F.A.M.E.*, was released in March 2011. The title stood for "Fans are my everything" and "Forgiving all my enemies." The album was a hit with fans and critics. It was his first album to reach number one on the *Billboard* 200 album chart. He had three hit singles on the album, "Yeah 3x," "Look at Me Now," and "Beautiful People." He worked with Lil Wayne, Busta Rhymes, Tyga, Ludacris, Benny Benassi, and Justin Bieber on the album. Some reviewers said it was Chris's best work. Chris went on tour across Australia and North America after the album was released.

Tina was still Chris's manager. They worked together to turn Chris's career around. He would avoid interviews and focus on performing. She said, "It was something we set a while back. We're not trying to be rude, selfish or disrespectful to anyone in any way. If people are going to judge anything, judge him for his talent. He signed up to sing and entertain. Not talk about his personal life." She continued, "We look at it as starting all over. Our grind, our choices are different than they probably would have been three years ago. But we are humbly trying to get back into the swing of things … He has a right to be able to grow up and learn about being a man, being a person."

The Winner

F.A.M.E. earned Chris Brown many nominations and awards. In June 2011 he was invited to the BET Awards. He had six nominations and won five: Best Male R&B Artist, Viewer's Choice Award, The Fandemonium Award, Best Collaboration, and Video of the Year. BET also had their hip-hop awards that year, and Chris won three awards there too. In November 2011 Chris was at the Soul Train Music Awards. *F.A.M.E.* won Album of the Year.

Chris's biggest comeback was at the Grammy Awards in February 2012. He had not appeared at the Grammy's since before he assaulted Rihanna. Chris was nominated for Best R&B Album, Best Rap Performance, and Best Rap Song. Chris was also invited to perform. He sang "Turn Up the Music" and "Beautiful People." And then he won his first Grammy for Best R&B Album. Chris tweeted after the show, "People who make mistakes and learn from them are role models too. I'm just happy to inspire growth and positivity."

Some viewers were very offended that Chris was welcomed back. The executive producer of the Grammy Awards said, "I think people deserve a second chance, you know." The producer then explained that the Grammy Awards were hurt by Chris's arrest since he was unable to perform the night he was charged with assault: "If you'll note, he has not been on the Grammys for the past few years and it may have taken us a while to kind of get over the fact that we were the victim of what happened."

Chris won a Grammy Award for Best R&B Album.

Singer Miranda Lambert was offended that Chris performed at the Grammys.

There were just as many people complaining that Chris appeared at the Grammy Awards. Country star Miranda Lambert tweeted during the awards, "He beat on a girl … not cool that we act like that didn't happen." Some music critics were offended that he was asked to perform. One said that everyone deserves a second chance. She added, "That doesn't mean they deserve a chance to strut around the Grammy stage a few years after being convicted of felony assault."

Chris stayed out of trouble during his probation. Because of this, Chris's lawyer asked that his probation and community service end. The judge in the case would not agree to this. Chris had only completed three months of his community service in two years. His sentence required that he perform six months of community service. The judge said it was not unreasonable to complete the sentence. The judge did agree to let Chris be closer to Rihanna. It allowed them to perform at the same events.

Oddly, Rihanna and Chris recorded two songs together in 2012. They recorded a version of her song "Birthday Cake" and a version of his song "Turn Up the Music." But weeks later, Chris *dissed* Rihanna in his song "Theraflu."

A few months later, Chris was injured in a fight in a New York City night club. Chris and the singer Drake were both in the club with friends. A fight broke out between the two groups. Eight people were injured. Drake and Chris blamed each other for starting the brawl. Both were sued for damages. The fight was supposedly over Rihanna.

Chris still keeps looking to the future. He released his fifth album, *Fortune*, in June 2012. He released five different singles from the album. Chris also performed on albums by Nicki Minaj, Brandy, Rick Ross, and David Guetta. When Chris appeared at live shows, huge crowds came to see him. Over 16,000 people showed up to see him sing a couple of songs on the *Today* show. Chris has gone back to acting too. He had a part in Steve Harvey's movie *Think Like a Man.* He also acted in the movies *Battle of the Year* and *Phenom.*

Another important part of Chris's life is being a mentor. He has reached out to Justin Bieber, another singer who found fame as a teen. Chris said, "He reminds me a lot of me when I was younger. I kind of try and be the big brother and make him go the right way and have a great time."

In addition to singing and acting, Chris started directing music videos. He made the video for Wale's song, "Slight Work." Wale said, "Me reaching out to Chris is bigger than me reaching out to a homeboy, it's me reaching out to an aspiring director. I think a lot of people put a lot of us into one box and don't know we have other passions. I wasn't surprised, a guy that creative and that talented, I'm sure he has other things that he wants to do." Chris is excited to start directing. He said, "My progression is to basically to be on the director's side and try to be behind the camera and creating a different world for people to see and be inspired."

Chris offered to help Justin Bieber adjust to becoming famous at such a young age.

Vocabulary

A&R	(adjective)	Artist and Repertoire; the division of a record company responsible for finding new talent
abusive	(adjective)	violent
Billboard	(noun)	magazine that covers the music industry, including record and album sales
CEO	(noun)	chief executive officer
contract	(noun)	an agreement between two people, between two companies, or between a person and a company
critic	(noun)	a person who judges
debut	(noun)	someone's first appearance
demo	(noun)	a sample, especially of a song, to introduce people to the musician
direct	(verb)	to guide the activities of others, such as in a performance
diss	(verb)	to insult
domestic violence	(noun)	violence against a person living in your own home or very close to you
entrepreneur	(noun)	a person who starts a new business
felony	(adjective)	a more serious form of a crime
genre	(noun)	a category of music, writing, or art
graffiti	(noun)	illegal drawings on public surfaces
Grammy Award	(noun)	an award given to the best recording artists every year
hip-hop	(adjective)	using strong beats and chanted words; music that uses strong beats and chanted words

hypocritical	(adjective)	acting as if one believes in certain values, but not really holding those values
lyrics	(noun)	words to a song
manager	(noun)	a person who does business on someone's behalf, a representative
mentor	(noun)	a wise or trusted teacher or counselor
mogul	(noun)	an important or wealthy person
nominate	(verb)	to suggest that someone might deserve an award
pop	(adjective)	generally appealing; a watered down version of rock and roll
probation	(noun)	a period of time when a criminal is supervised by the court
producer	(noun)	a person who raises money to create a song, a stage show, and so on
promote	(verb)	to sell or advertise for a product
rap	(adjective or noun)	spoken with rhythm; to speak with rhythm; music in which words are spoken in rhythm
single	(noun)	one song, usually from an album
soul	(adjective)	the combined sound of rhythm and blues and gospel
tweet	(verb)	to post a message on the social media website Twitter

Picture Credits